AF371341

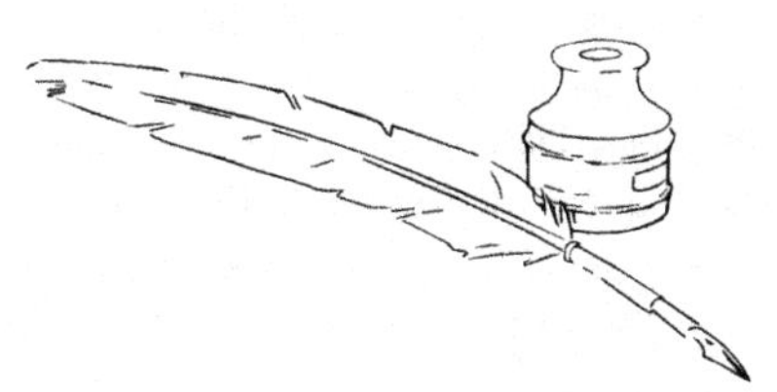

Published by Canon Press
P.O. Box 8729, Moscow, Idaho 83843
800.488.2034 | www.canonpress.com

Brian Brown, *Worldview Guide for Walden*
Copyright © 2019 by Brian Brown.
For the Canon Classics edition of the novel go to www.canonpress.com/books/
canon-classics.

Cover design by James Engerbretson
Cover illustration by Forrest Dickison
Interior design by Valerie Anne Bost and James Engerbretson

Printed in the United States of America.

A free end-of-book test and answer key are available for download at
www.canonpress.com/ClassicsQuizzes

Library of Congress Cataloging-in-Publication Data:
Brown, Brian, 1977- author.
Worldview guide : Walden / Brian Brown.
Walden
Moscow, Idaho : Canon Press, [2019] | Audience: Grades 7-9
LCCN 2019039774 | ISBN 9781947644267 (paperback)
LCSH: Thoreau, Henry David, 1817-1862. Walden—Juvenile
   literature. | Christianity in literature—Juvenile literature.
Classification: LCC PS3048 .B76 2019 | DDC 818/.303—dc23
LC record available at https://lccn.loc.gov/2019039774

19 20 21 22 23 24   9 8 7 6 5 4 3 2 1

WORLDVIEW GUIDE

WALDEN

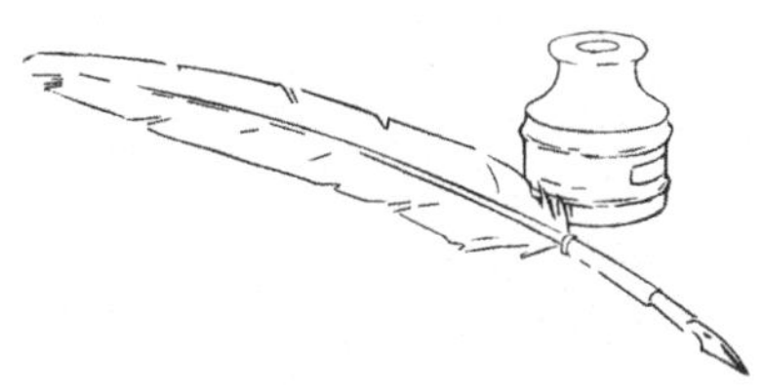

Brian Brown

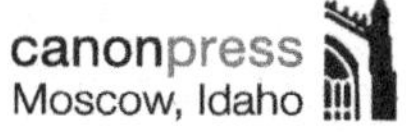

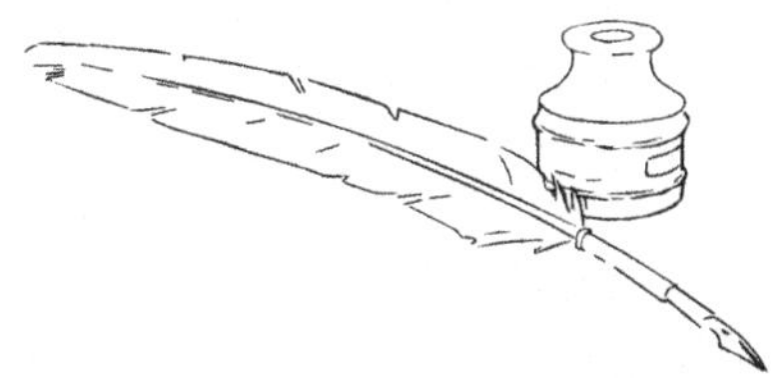

CONTENTS

INTRODUCTION

Love your life, poor as it is. [1]

Walden is a book that defies traditional classification. Thoreau moves nimbly between social commentary, political critique and vivid descriptions of the parenting behavior of wood-cocks. His assessment of his modern society is at once insightful and boorish. He identifies with piercing accuracy the enslavement of his fellow citizens to the complexities of modern life while neglecting the many gifts that are given to us in and through the City of Man. *Walden* offers the insight of a man who sees the beauty of the world and the growing ugliness of an emerging modern American society.

---

1. All citatiden are to *Walden: 150th Anniversary Edition* (Princeton, NJ: Princeton University Press, 2004), 328.

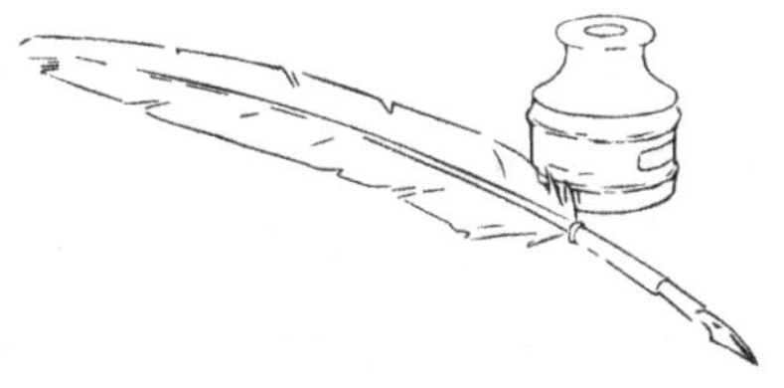

THE WORLD AROUND

Thoreau published *Walden* in 1854, almost a decade after beginning his experiment in the woods. Rationalism and the Enlightenment had given birth to a whole new world of discontent as the new American republic began to define itself. The foment of numerous social reform movements, such as abolitionism, was just one way that the young nation was attempting to break free from the old world of Europe. The young nation had grown over its first 50 years into an adolescent struggling to figure out exactly what she would be socially, philosophically and culturally. In a few years the outbreak of the Civil War would bring the divergent cultures of North and South into conflict, raise the great evil of slavery to the forefront of our nation's consciousness and forge a new national identity.

The philosophical movement of the Enlightenment had begun to transform the way Americans and Europeans viewed and interacted with the world. It began as a rejection of the wisdom of the ages (notably a rejection of the Church's authority) and a redefinition of the person in radically individualistic terms. The world born of the Enlightenment—a modern, cold, closed world bounded by scientific rationalism and marked by marginalized deity—was shaping the soul of the young country. In New England, the Puritan roots of America had largely been rejected. Rationalism was king. And while the Unitarians stretched to try and introduce a religion able to survive in this new world, the transcendentalists were concerned that we still found ourselves isolated from whatever it was that made the world magical, beautiful, and true. Ralph Waldo Emerson, along with his transcendentalist brothers and sisters, was imagining a world beyond the rational and observable, free from the constraints of a merely orthodox and historic Christianity. The growing movement of transcendentalism, which began as a Romantic philosophical movement, soon became a literary one, and significantly influenced the religious landscape of the new country. Thoreau, and his work *Walden*, stand as a unique and influential representative of that new sort of literature. It was an attempt to kick against the goads of a cold modern world without going back to the gods (or God) of the old world.

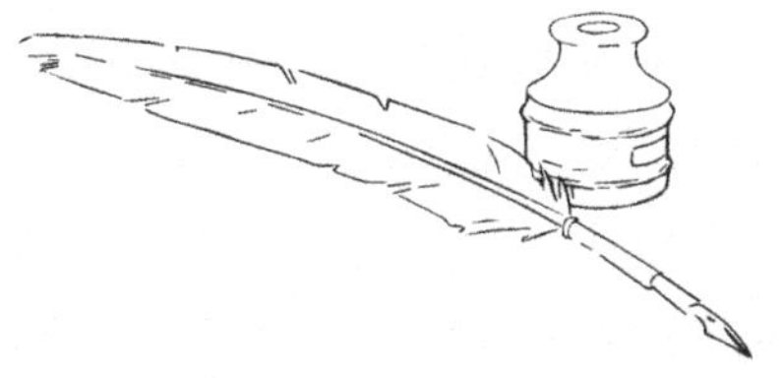

ABOUT THE AUTHOR

Henry David Thoreau was born in the middle of these historical and social movements in Concord, Massachusetts in 1817. His childhood was spent in and around Concord, including in the woods surrounding the small town. Boarders frequented his home while his father ran a moderately successful pencil factory. He studied at Harvard College where he focused on Greek and Latin. After school he helped his brother start a school and worked with his father in the pencil factory. Neither career stuck. He moved on from both school and industry towards a life of philosophy, leisure and writing. He soon found his way to the tutelage of Ralph Waldo Emerson and was immersed in the ideas of transcendentalism. Transcendentalism was a philosophical and literary movement grounded in a theology that placed the divine within the confines of the natural world and each human individual.

The influence of transcendentalism pushed Thoreau towards the natural world—a world he'd always been drawn to. And while he never permanently left Concord, Massachusetts, he traveled broadly, enjoying, observing and searching creation. It was in creation, the transcendentalists believed, that man would find the insight necessary to define wisdom, joy and whatever ethical norms could be discovered. Emerson's influence on Thoreau was profound. Henry lived with the Emersons, and the experiment of *Walden* took place on their land.

Many of Thoreau's early writings were initially published through the transcendentalist paper, *The Week*. He was an essayist and engaged many of the social issues of his day. He wrote *Civil Disobedience* after spending an evening in jail when he refused to pay a poll tax in protest of the government's protection of slavery. He believed that he had a moral obligation to refuse to pay taxes to a government that protected such an institution. Such a practice ran counter to some of Thoreau's most deeply held convictions, including the transcendentalist emphasis on self-reliance and the presence of the divine within the individual. He and his family participated in the Underground Railroad by smuggling escaped slaves from the South to Canada through their family home.

After his experiment in the woods, Thoreau returned to city life in Concord. His cabin in the woods was given to another family. Thoreau died of a tuberculosis infection at the age of 44. While his writings were locally known and influential among the other transcendentalists, *Walden* brought Thoreau fame after his death in 1862, eight years after it was published.

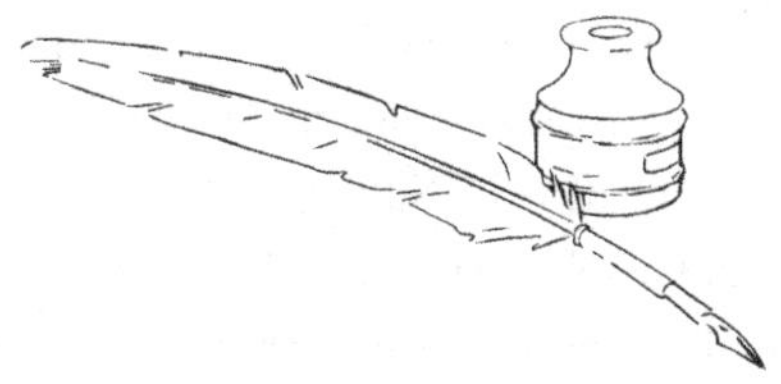

WHAT OTHER NOTABLES SAID

Walden was warmly received in Thoreau's time, but during the decades following his death it grew in influence markedly. A number of critics described *Walden* as cranky and Thoreau's own lifestyle as lacking necessary ambition. But the growth of a modern and complex technological society has led to increasing numbers of people looking for Thoreau's own insights on how to live in that society. The influence of *Walden* on American literature is massive. Robert Frost wrote that "in one book … he surpasses everything we have had in America."[2]

While E.B. White summarized the work well, writing:

> If Thoreau had merely left us an account of a man's
> life in the woods or if he had simply retreated to
> the woods and there recorded his complaints about

2. Robert Frost, "Letter to Wade Van Gore," June 24, 1922, in *Twentieth Century Interpretations of Walden*, ed. Richard Ruland. Prentice Hall (Upper Saddle River, NJ: Prentice Hall Direct, 1968).

society, or even if he had contrived to include both records in one essay, *Walden* would probably not have lived a hundred years. As things turned out, Thoreau, very likely without knowing quite what he was up to, took man's relation to Nature and man's dilemma in society and man's capacity for elevating his spirit and he beat all these matters together, in a wild free interval of self-justification and delight, and produced an original omelette from which people can draw nourishment in a hungry day.[3]

Critics have always noted Thoreau's grumpiness towards the surrounding society. But almost everyone identifies the uniqueness of Thoreau's work. John Updike, in a recently published introduction to the work, writes of Thoreau and *Walden's* influence on our day:

> A century and a half after its initial publication, *Walden* has become such a totem of the back-to-nature, preservationist, anti-business, civil-disobedience mind-set, and Thoreau so vivid a protester, so perfect a crank and hermit saint, that the book itself risks being as revered and unread as the Bible.[4]

Walden is a book born of America's adolescent literary and philosophical days. It has both marked the time in which it was written and shaped the world into which it was sent. Within a few decades, its importance had become apparent as more and more readers were drawn to

---

3. E.B. White, *Essays of E. B. White* (New York: HarperCollins, 2006), 293-294.

4. *Walden: 150th Anniversary Edition*, ix.

the seemingly alternative sort of world that Thoreau called us to into.

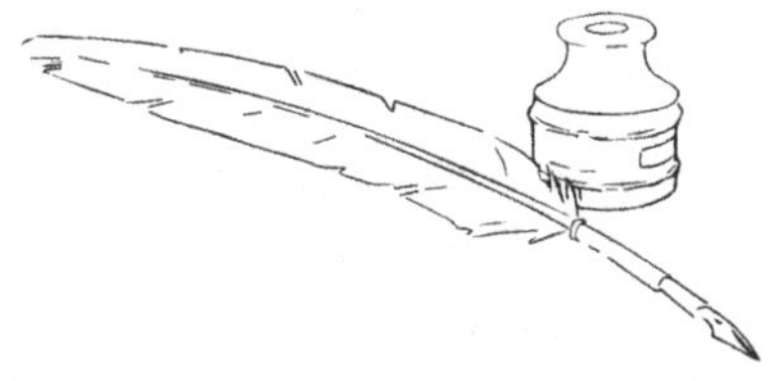

SETTING, CHARACTERS
AND PLOT SUMMARY

Walden is Thoreau's account of what he termed an "experiment" during which time he lived in the woods surrounding Walden Pond for 2 years, 2 months and 2 days. It doesn't fit well under any particular genre. It addresses philosophy on one page and walks through the costs of building a house on the next. It addresses the woes of society while debating the depth and area of a pond. It attempts to represent the lived experiment of transcendentalist philosophy in the mundane realities of everyday life in nature. *Walden* sits nowhere neatly. It presents a distinctive worldview, but it eschews excessive philosophical explanation and instead gives practical descriptions of a self-reliant life.

Much of the book reads as a sort of journal entry. Thoreau loosely follows the seasons of a year as an outline for his book, using those seasons as way of observing the world and describing his daily life on the pond. We encounter the wildlife surrounding the pond in the nearby woods. We meet transients who come to fish or live nearby. Thoreau informs us of some of the historical characters who resided near the pond. But what we meet most directly is Thoreau's eyes. Reading *Walden* is an exercise in learning to see the world anew through the vision and observations of a man committed to living a particular kind of life (at least for a season) in the wood near Walden Pond and away from the bustle and life offered in Concord.

The normal characters surrounding Concord are thus transformed through Thoreau's vision. Farmers become slaves. Shop owners, selling their wares, are Odysseus' mermaids. The wildlife becomes Thoreau's neighbors. But the center of *Walden* is observation. Thoreau watches, he measures, he assesses, contemplates. To read *Walden* is to watch the world.

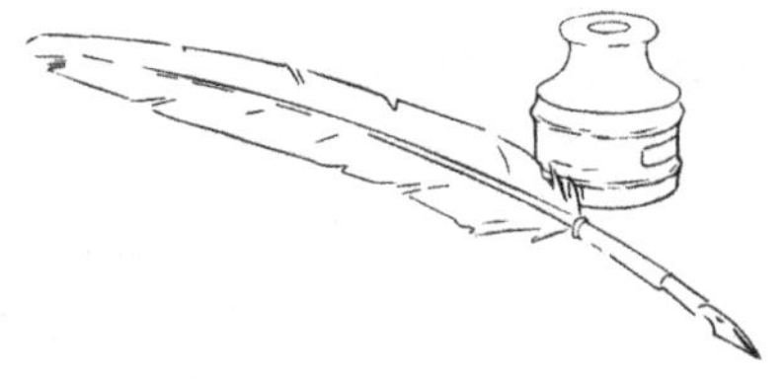

WORLDVIEW ANALYSIS

Walden sets out to live an experiment. Thoreau moves to the woods outside of Concord to put a worldview into practice. What one finds of theory in *Walden* is so intricately tied to the actual practice of living described in its pages that there is little opportunity to meditate too long without immediately getting to the business of day-to-day life. Before we evaluate Thoreau's worldview, we should take time to admire the strength of his commitment to it. This is no theoretical treatise. It is an experiment, described, reflected on and *lived*. As those who hold to a Christian worldview, we should feel powerfully the challenge laid at our feet by Thoreau. Many of his problems with Christianity were not simply objections to its ideas, but to the failure of its proponents to truly embody those ideas in practice. Thoreau's emphasis on a real and lived philosophy is vital to understanding his work in *Walden*.

Thoreau was steeped in the transcendentalist belief that the natural world provids a lens, perhaps the only lens, through which divine reality can be seen and known. But in *Walden* Thoreau goes further and approaches the natural world as actually indwelt by the divine. For Emerson and his followers, one looks to the trees to learn something of the ways of god and the world. But in Thoreau, one looks to the trees to see something of god himself. While the transcendentalists embraced a kind of natural revelation closely related to the Christian worldview, Thoreau's Christianity is swallowed up by a Hindu-influenced pantheism. Thoreau's thought was heavily shaped by the Bhagavad Gita and other Hindu writings that had been recently translated into English and made accessible to a broader European and American readership. Thoreau's pantheism reduced god to a kind of bland aesthetic and philosophical ideal. There was no person creating and acting and moving in the world. There is, for Thoreau, only an impersonal principle—vague and illusive, often hidden from view by the society we labor so hard to build.

It is here in Thoreau's most problematic philosophical assumptions that we encounter some of his most insightful writing. He observes the world with an attentiveness that Scripture calls us to. This attentiveness to the world runs through the whole of *Walden*, often appearing in the most interesting of places. In Thoreau, observing nature is an end unto itself. This leads to an implicit tension between the poetic and the "scientific." The transcendentalists represented a response to a modern materialism that had drained the world of all magic and wonder. While they had no intentions of returning to the old world of religious superstition, the pursuit of transcendence in the midst of the world of the senses defined their movement. The attentiveness we see in *Walden* was an attention derived from this pursuit.

Thoreau describes the mating rituals of insects, the work habits of ants, and the accumulation of snowfall with a great deal of precision. He sketches detailed maps of the shape and depth of Walden Pond. He is pressed to observe the most mundane of details *and* to consider their implications for human life. Nature itself teaches us how to live and reveals the character and will of God. It is Thoreau's attentiveness to these realities that drives him to the woods in the first place. He is exasperated by the noise that surrounds life in society—the endless complications that leave men further and further distant from nature and one another.

And this is precisely where Thoreau's work has much to commend itself, particularly for those of us who worship the God who has made this world. Thoreau sees around him a world flooded with beauty and goodness, and while he abandons the good he might have discovered around him in the work of the farmer and miller in town, he calls us to rediscover the *whatness* of the trees, the insects and other natural phenomena that surround us each day.

Thoreau subverts society's predominant answer to the question of how much is enough. Again and again, Thoreau does not think we need very much at all. In "Economy" he humorously describes some townsmen's acquisition of farm equipment as a significant misfortune. Whereas we tend to equate financial production with freedom, Thoreau sees the opposite. He views the addition of more and more stuff and the accompanying financial complexity as slavery. We work to acquire things which require work to maintain and use which all amounts to an increased amount of required work. Our things don't give us the good life: they keep us from it. Thoreau's experiment is a call to question this fundamental assertion that undergirds much of our living.

As far as the question of *what it means for man to have true knowledge,* Thoreau is content, in most places, to leave us with vague platitudes and a commitment to simplicity for the sake of leisure and attentiveness. In other words, while Thoreau is committed to pursuing knowledge of the world, it is not so much a propositional understanding of what is true so much as a kind of simple, unencumbered life that experiences that knowledge. Awareness of the physical world around us is the foundation for all of Thoreau's philosophy and ethics. Everything that distracts or pulls man away from this awareness is bad, and everything that enhances this sort of life is good. In *Walden,* awareness is knowledge. Thoreau wants his readers to not only notice the world around them, but also to attend to its uniqueness. It is not enough to be aware of the brightness of the sun as it rises, but we should also know both what the sun is made of and what it is. Awareness is a vital aspect to living in the world, but it should be in the service of knowledge.

As Christians, Thoreau's disregard for the Bible is troubling, and yet his intentionality with regards to the created world fits beautifully with how creation is described throughout Scripture. Paul tells us in Romans 1 that God has made Himself known through the things He has made, and David declares in Psalm 19 that the heavens declare the glory of God. Thoreau's regard for the created world takes these biblical claims with the utmost seriousness. While such knowledge is insufficient, it is true and valuable. This knowledge should be pursued by all who love the Creating God who is revealed in Scripture, without abandoning the priority of Scripture as the center of God's revealed word.

On the other hand, underlying Thoreau's work is a strong bifurcation between the "natural world" and the worlds of the farmer, the merchant and society generally. While he helps us to see the beauty and wisdom in the lives of insects and the growth of trees, he fails to see the marvels and gifts that surround him in Concord. The world cannot be neatly divided between God's gifts in creation and the gifts He gives through the growth of culture. The cultivation of creation by man can be as remarkable and beautiful as what's to be found in the woods around Walden Pond. As Luther has famously reminded us, God provides us milk through the diligence of the milkmaid.

Walden was an experiment in living a life of self-sufficiency. The truly human life for Thoreau was a life built with one's own hands, free from the slavery of needing either the conveniences of modern life or the service of others. Thoreau moved to the woods, recycled lumber from another plot of land to build his cabin, and grew or caught his own food. He lived a simple life, what he might describe as a truly free life. This kind of life, one of *real* self-sufficiency, is the good life according to Thoreau. He goes to great lengths, in the opening chapters of *Walden*, not to describe the why of his experiment so much as to describe the economics of his decision. He charts how little it cost him to embark on the two years, and how little he truly needed in order to survive. And it is in this economics that we glimpse both Thoreau's vision of the good life and the underlying purpose of his experiment. The good life can be had for very little, in fact it may *only* be found with very little.

This explains some of his vehement hatred of the institution of slavery. It is on the grounds of this self-sufficiency and freedom that he opposes the government's defense of it. One's livelihood should not depend on the enslavement of others. Such a life represents the most reprehensible abandonment of Thoreau's good life.

The problem with adopting such a radical notion of self-sufficiency is that, even at Thoreau's most "free," he is still highly dependent on the society around him. He lives on another's land, he depends on commerce in the city for many of his daily needs, and his vision of a self-sufficient and deeply individualistic life is untenable. Men and women were made for society. We are interdependent creatures whose lives in the world can never be completely self-sufficient. For all of *Walden's* noble pretensions, Thoreau cannot escape his own humanity. Men will always need the work and the community of other men.

To be sure, self-sufficiency doesn't require a lone cabin in the woods, and Thoreau would live out the rest of his days very much intertwined with the society of Concord, but his two years at Walden would serve as a test, a kind of experiment for transcendentalist ideas and for what sort of self-sufficiency was possible. One of the questions that undergirds this work is the question of how much of the complexity of life can be eliminated. Thoreau understands the good that comes as a result of modern society. He expresses comfort at the sound of a passing train and the industry it represents. While this may seem inconsistent with his other complaints, it is important to remember that Thoreau's goals are not all-or-nothing. His goal is for men to slow their assumed trajectory towards greater and greater industry and complexity and to consider what they have gained as well as what is lost in the expansion of technology and its attendant complexity. He wants this growth to be minimized or slowed. It is as if the business of town life and work are noise, drowning out the pristine life of simplicity and the voice of the divine to be heard in the natural world. If Thoreau was deeply troubled by the materialism and noise of his own day, then one can only imagine his response to the growth of these things in our own day.

As Christians, there is much value in the work we are called to do in the world—a work that isn't simply concerned with self-sufficiency but with the cultivation of a worldwide garden-city, such as we see at the end of the book of Revelation. We are called not simply to grow food or build houses for ourselves, but to cultivate the things God has placed in the world for the flourishing of our neighbor. While the spiritual dangers of materialism and the envy that can so easily accompany it are real, there is an aspect of our humanity that exists for the sake of honoring God in this work. The good life does not just consist of avoiding slavery to material goods, but also includes receiving with thanksgiving everything that God has given us in this world.

Where Thoreau pushes for simplicity and utility in our approach to food and shelter, the Scriptures view wine and rich food as good gifts from God: "Bread is made for laughter, and wine gladdens life, and money answers everything" (Eccl. 10:19). Thoreau raises valid concerns about our tendency to become enslaved to work and material things. The Bible warns us differently though. It is a warning aimed at ingratitude or selfishness, not a warning against the goods themselves (Rom. 1:21). Whereas materialism leads us to believe that the goods themselves lead us to the good life, and Thoreau's approach leads us to believe that they distract us or even keep us from the good life, the Bible points to these goods as one of the products of a life well lived.

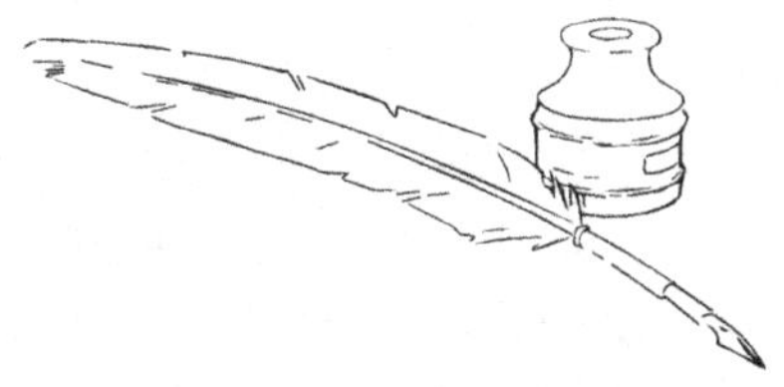

QUOTABLES

1. "Children, who play life, discern its true law and relations more clearly than men, who fail to live it worthily, but who think that they are wiser by experience, that is, by failure." (p. 96)

2. "Be it life or death, we crave only reality. If we are really dying, let us hear the rattle in our throats and feel cold in the extremities; if we are alive, let us go about our business." (p. 98)

3. "With a little more deliberation in the choice of their pursuits, all men would perhaps become essentially students and observers, for certainly their nature and destiny are interesting to all alike. In accumulating property for ourselves or our posterity, in founding a family or a state, or acquiring fame even, we are mortal; but in dealing with truth we are immortal, and need fear no change nor accident." (p. 99)

4. "I went to the woods because I wished to live deliberately, to front only the essential facts of life, and see if I could not learn what it had to teach, and not, when I came to die, discover that I had not lived. I did not wish to live what was not life, living is so dear; nor did I wish to practice resignation, unless it was quite necessary. I wanted to live deep and suck out all the marrow of life, to live so sturdily and Spartan-like as to put to rout all that was not life, to cut a broad swath and shave close, to drive life into a corner, and reduce it to its lowest terms, and, if it proved to be mean, why then to get the whole and genuine meanness of it, and publish its meanness to the world; or if it were sublime, to know it by experience, and be able to give a true account of it in my next excursion." (p. 90-91)

5. "Rather than love, than money, than fame, give me truth." (p. 330)

6. "Every generation laughs at the old fashions, but follows religiously the new." (p. 26)

7. "However mean your life is, meet and live it; do not shun it and call it hard names. It is not so bad as you are. It looks poorest when you are richest. The fault-finder will find faults even in paradise. Love your life, poor as it is. You may perhaps have some pleasant, thrilling, glorious hours, even in a poorhouse. The setting sun is reflected from the windows of the almshouse as brightly as from the rich man's abode; the snow melts before its doors as early in the spring. Cultivate property like a garden

herb, like sage. Do not trouble yourself much to get new things, whether clothes or friends. Turn the old; return to them. Things do not change; we change. Sell your clothes and keep your thoughts… Superfluous wealth can buy superfluities only. Money is not required to buy one necessary of the soul." (p. 328-329)

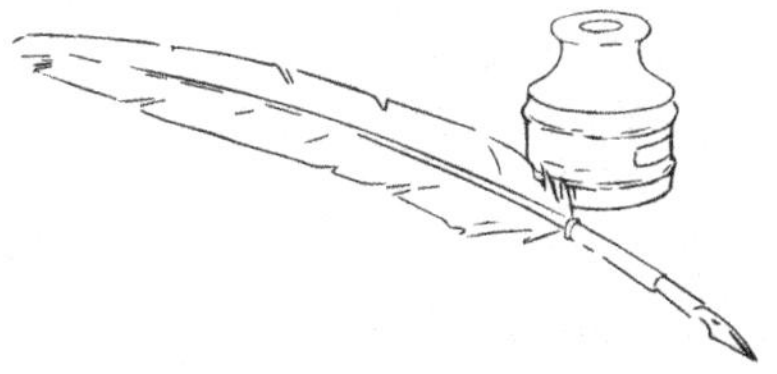

21 SIGNIFICANT QUESTIONS AND ANSWERS

1. What is Thoreau's goal in living in the woods?

> He states that he goes to the woods because he wished to live deliberately. Thoreau believes that much of human life is spent in a kind of sleep or, to use another metaphor, in a quiet desperation. *Walden* represented Thoreau's attempt to experience as much life as he could—life without most of the comforts and busy-ness that seem to numb the human soul to what life really is. He does not go to escape pain or reality, but to taste the raw experience of life in his bones. For Thoreau, much of modern life was lived far above the craggy realities of nature and therefore far out of earshot of all that nature might have to say to us concerning the good life. Thoreau went to live the life that nature could offer, or at least to get as close as he possibly could.

2. How did Thoreau provide for his needs? How was he
    employed?

> Thoreau used a relatively meager sum of money to
> begin his experiment. He details his costs and in-
> come in the chapter "Economy." He built his cabin
> for 28 dollars and 12.5 cents. He met most of his ex-
> penses through farming and selling some portion of
> the crop that he did not eat. One of the goals of his
> experiment was to gain time for leisurely contem-
> plation. It represented a rather perfect example of
> something Thoreau's friend Ralph Waldon Emerson
> critiqued him for: a general lack of ambition.

3. Does Thoreau believe in such a thing as moral virtues?

> Thoreau is no moral relativist. *Walden* is filled with
> examples of his moral opinions. Slavery is con-
> demned. A life spent in slavery to taste or fashion
> or labor is condemned. Thoreau resists many of the
> compromises necessitated by living within a demo-
> cratic and an economically mobile society. What re-
> mains less clear for the reader of *Walden* is Thoreau's
> source of authority for these moral judgments.

4. How do we discover moral virtues?

> The discovery of moral virtues, as well as growth
> in their practice, is largely gained through the con-
> templation of the natural world and a life lived in
> accordance with what one observes. If this seems a
> bit vague, it is. But for Thoreau the "noise" of life had
> brought a complexity that kept mankind hurried, am-

bitious and kept from the substance of life itself. As he says in several places, "Simplify! Simplify! Simplify!"

5.   Why did Thoreau stop living in the woods?

According to Thoreau, that life had ended and another needed to begin. It is important to see his time at *Walden* not as a desired permanent state, but truly as a temporary experiment. He is not recommending such a life for all, but rather spends a season observing what such a life might do to and for himself.

6.   Why does Thoreau dwell on such mundane details such as the feeding pattern of chickadees, the depth of the pond and the songs of woodcocks?

These details represent in *Walden* wonderful realities that we miss in our pursuit of more. They are more than bare facts: they also instruct us about the very nature of life and the beauty of the world we live in.

7.   In *Walden*, does Thoreau oppose all industry and modern advancements?

No. He is comforted by the representative sound of industry passing by in the sound of a train or a wagon carrying goods. His challenge is not against the existence of industry or material advancements, but rather he continues to question how much of this is truly an advancement for humanity and how these advancements in fact dull the senses and do not lead to individual flourishing.

8. How is *Walden* structured?

    Walden compresses two years on the pond into a single year, using the seasons of the year as a kind of basic structure on which he hangs his observations and philosophy. The structure is very loose, but important. Thoreau's other published book, *A Week on the Concord and Merrimack Rivers*, received criticism both for its preachiness and its meandering lack of structure.

9. Where was Thoreau's cabin? Is this guy a hermit?

    Thoreau's cabin was only a short walk from the town of Concord. Walden Pond was a popular destination for picnicking, swimming and natural recreation for the townspeople. Thoreau was not isolated from people, and that was never his intention. His goal was to reduce the surrounding noise and material possessions, not to simply "rough it." His home saw regular visitors from town (some desired, others not) and he had three chairs—"one for solitude, two for friendship, and three for society."

10. How did the community in Concord respond to this experiment?

    Concord mostly responded with curiosity. Thoreau saw regular visitors from town who came to visit Thoreau's cabin on the pond.

11. When did Thoreau write *Walden*, and why did he take 10 years to publish the work?

   Walden was originally written as a series of observations about the world. After *A Week on the Concord and Merrimack Rivers* failed to reach much of an audience, Thoreau took extended time to impose a more comprehensible structure onto *Walden*.

12. If I wanted to know the depth of Walden Pond, would *Walden* be a good place to discover this information?

   Yes. While Walden Pond was rumored to have no bottom whatsoever, Thoreau set out to measure the depth and size of the pond. In the chapter, "The Pond in Winter," Thoreau details how he took soundings of the depth of the pond in a systematic way to determine its maximum depth. He accurately determined that the pond at its deepest point was 107 feet deep.

13. What does Thoreau do with his hardships?

   "Love your life, poor as it is..." He seeks to relish in whatever it is that comes his way. He casts aside most materialistic measures of the good life in favor of a life unencumbered and undistracted by complexity. He seems to desire, more than anything, to feel and experience fully all that may come his way. His observations of the poor in Concord is that they, in many important ways, experience a far more independent (and thus richer) life than the wealthy merchants or farmers. The measure of a life is not its comforts, but its self-sufficiency.

14. Who is God for Thoreau in *Walden*?

God is impersonal, mystical and barely discernible throughout *Walden*. While the world is shot through with the divine, it is not a divinity that can be known or is personal in the Christian sense. It is a concept of god heavily influenced by Hinduism and American Unitarianism. Thoreau, like other transcendentalists, was reacting against the scientific materialism of his day, but would not return to an older religious worldview. Instead, the movement devised an American Platonic religion that celebrated the mystical beyond the natural world, that this natural world somehow ambiguously reflected. There are portions of *Walden* that reflect a rather negative view of physical pleasures (one thinks of Thoreau's reflections on food and sex), while other portions that seem to celebrate the natural world in glowing terms. Numerous scholars have noted Thoreau's distinctiveness in comparison to other transcendentalists like Emerson. Whereas the gulf between the natural world and the divine is heavily emphasized in other transcendentalists, Thoreau sees much more correlation between the world around us and the divine. Whoever god is in *Walden*, he is not a person as much as a divine ideal to be seen through and in the midst of the natural world.

15. Did Thoreau have any visitors while living in the woods?

> He often had visitors to his cabin. The pond itself was a popular location for residents of Concord to picnic, fish and swim. It was only a half hour's walk from town. Thoreau mentions returning to his cabin after hikes in the wood to find that there had been uninvited visitors in his home while he was gone. Family friends and townspeople would frequently visit Thoreau's cabin to socialize and observe the sort of life he was enjoying there.

16. How long did Thoreau live in the woods?

> Thoreau lived at Walden from July 1845 to September 1847. During the two years and two months that he lived on the pond, he took several trips to other places around New England, including a trip to visit Mount Katahdin in Maine. After leaving his cabin in the woods, he resided in Ralph Waldo Emerson's home for two years while Emerson was in Europe.

17. How did Thoreau use up his time while living in the woods?

> Thoreau kept busy with all manner of work and leisure. He grew food, some of which he ate and some of which he sold or traded. He spent time reading and writing. He describes in relative detail the process he followed in cleaning his cabin—first emptying the entirety of his possessions onto the grass in front of his cabin and then cleaning the inside (he observed an odd sort of pleasure at seeing all of his

furniture out-of-doors). But he spent a great deal of time in leisurely contemplation: observing, measuring, thinking about the life surrounding the pond in the woods. It was the relative simplicity of his life that freed him for this sort of life in the woods.

18. Does Thoreau believe that we should all go live like he did?

No. But he does believe that we should all simplify our lives in the direction that he did. He sees the overwhelming problem in the world as being abundance, not a lack. We do not need more stuff; we need less. We do not need better and greater quantities of food; we need less. His time in the woods represented an extreme example of this, and while he would never require such a life he does believe that men should move towards increasing simplicity.

19. What does Thoreau eat? Why?

Thoreau goes into great detail into how he set up his garden. He ate a great deal of beans, with some other vegetables and corn. As with everything else in Thoreau's life, his diet was extremely simple. He even describes trapping and eating a woodchuck who was raiding his bean garden. Thoreau's concern was to reduce what many consider the necessities of living. A complex diet leads to all sorts of other necessary complexities. These complexities inevitably ensnare men as they become slaves to the work that sustains such a life.

20. What does Thoreau think of the newspaper and the mail?

> "To a philosopher all news, as it is called, is gossip, and they who edit and read it are old women over their tea." He has little use for either. He claims to have only received two letters in his life that "… were worth the postage."[5] Thoreau's understanding of what actually amounts to significant news simply doesn't occur very often. Instead men fill their minds and their time contemplating trivia that has little or no real significance for their lives and for the world, while neglecting the more immediate and mundane realities in which their lives are immersed.

21. Thoreau doesn't seem bothered by being lost. How does his attitude towards being lost in the woods demonstrate a different set of values than what is mostly adhered to in modern society?

> Emerson criticized Thoreau for lacking some of the basic ambitions that drove most of his neighbors. Thoreau lived much of his life meandering. He wasn't troubled by being lost because he had eliminated almost all sense of hurry from his life. In *Walden*, he delights in a night spent "feeling" his way through the woods back to his cabin after the sun had gone down and there was almost no light with which to find his way. He believes there is much to see, enjoy and learn from at each step along the way. The important thing is to observe and to contemplate, not simply to arrive.

---

5. *Walden: 150th Anniversary Edition*, 94.

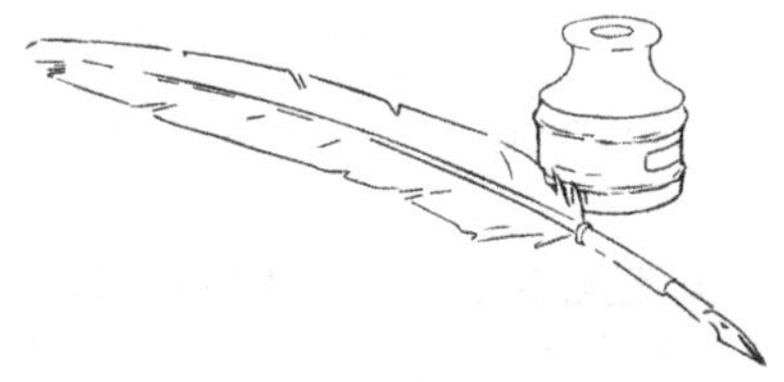

FURTHER DISCUSSION AND REVIEW

Master what you have read by reviewing and integrating the different elements of this classic.

HISTORICAL AND PHILOSOPHICAL CONTEXT

Be prepared to discuss and consider the connections between the emerging American literary identity, Romanticism and transcendentalism and Thoreau's own adaptation and place in these historical and philosophical movements. What sets *Walden* apart? Why is the book's historical context significant as we consider it as a religious and philosophical work?

CRITIQUE OF SOCIETY

Walden has been criticized as being excessively preachy and Thoreau as too curmudgeonly in his observations of his neighbors and townspeople. Consider how some of

Thoreau's concerns about technological developments and wealth have become characteristically true in our age. What holes do you see in his thinking?

WALDEN AS A CALL TO OBSERVE THE CREATED WORLD

Thoreau places a premium on a life spent contemplating the natural world and the lives of our neighbors. What parts of a biblical understanding of the world are strongly reinforced by this emphasis in *Walden*? What aspects are neglected or treated insufficiently by this emphasis on natural revelation?

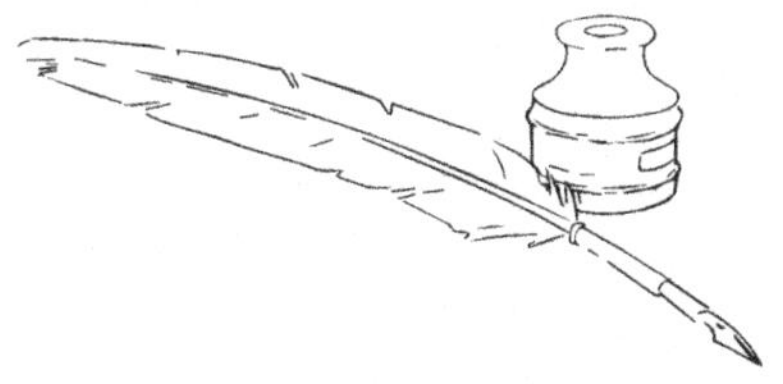# A NOTE FROM THE PUBLISHER:
TAKING THE CLASSICS QUIZ

Once you have finished the worldview guide, you can prepare for the end-of-book test. Each test will consist of a short-answer section on the book itself and the author, a short-answer section on plot and the narrative, and a long-answer essay section on worldview, conflict, and themes.

Each quiz, along with other helps, can be downloaded for free at www.canonpress.com/ClassicsQuizzes. If you have any questions about the quiz or its answers or the Worldview Guides in general, you can contact Canon Press at service@canonpress.com or 208.892.8074.

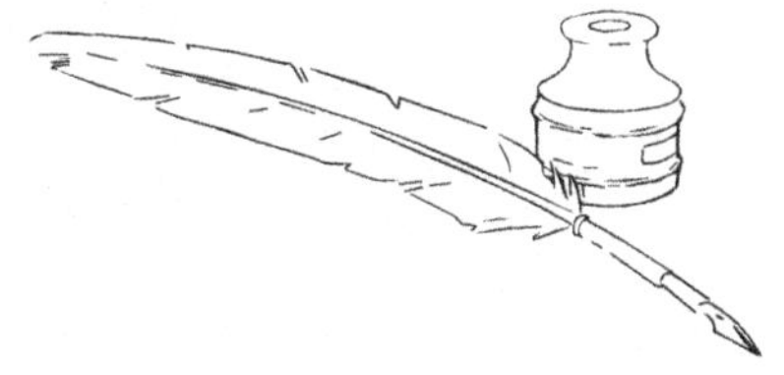

ABOUT THE AUTHOR

Brian Brown is pastor at Trinity Church Denver and a founding board member at Augustine Classical Academy, where all three of his children are enrolled. He got a Master's degree in biblical exegesis at Wheaton.

Made in the USA
Monee, IL
07 July 2026

56546302R00038